Vol. 1

FART POETRY

Bad vibrations

Everybody felt the ripples,

soon will come the stench.

Who could be the secret farter

sitting on the bench?

Veteran airy bum

Here's advice for windy people:
train to be a vet.
If you fart in front of clients,
blame it on their pet!

IBS-capades

Oft' I go on flights of whimsy,
dreaming of a bowel not flimsy.
In my mind I'm fearless, free,
lord of my reality.
I could take the starring role,
not sidekick to my bum hole.

Christmas heave

When Father Christmas visits you,

he pulls his presents down the flue.

Placing them beneath the tree,

he holds his breath

and counts to three.

Rumbling comes from his gut.

Pressure builds behind his butt.

Letting off a giant fart,

it's time for Santa to depart.

Ghostly essence

If you want to catch a ghost
the witching hour is best.
Stay awake on Halloween
and try this simple test.

Sit inside a darkened room,
close your eyes and ears.
Concentrate on any smells
leaked from ghostly rears.

Ghosts can't touch or make a noise.
Ghosts cannot be seen.
Farting is the only way
you'll know where ghosts have been.

Cheeky rumble

There are many different farts
escaping from my bum.
I cannot predict from which
direction they will come.

Some will rumble up the cheeks,
others spit and splutter.
They're so unpredictable
my arse smells like a gutter.

Love stinks

Don't stand upwind on a date,
it isn't very smart.
Sure, it's true that love is blind,
but it can smell a fart.

Love guff air

If you are a lonely heart,

why not marry your own fart?

You can share your life together,

just remember, check the weather!

Should it be a windy day,

it could blow your love away.

Up the aisle

If only I could wed my arse,
and call it my own Mrs.
We'd be happy, arse and I,
until it blew me kisses.

Trapped wind

Sliding out of bed a morning
after too much booze,
takes a lot of effort when you'd
really rather snooze.

Soon your tummy grumbles and
you scramble for the loo.
Last night's drunken snack is now
a monumental poo.

Emptied of the load, it's back
to bed where you discover,
smelly clouds of fart that you
set free from 'neath the cover.

Inter-smeller travel

If I were an astronaut
I'd float around in space,
launching gasses from my bum
to get from place to place.

Hippo bottom gas

All the creatures at the zoo
are frightened of the hippo.
They will run the other way
in case it lets one rippo.

Pipe down

Let me offer some advice;

a useful quiet trump device.

If you pull your cheeks apart,

you should do a silent fart.

Pooper hero

I can brew a giant fart
and fire it from my eyes.
Drinking lots of lemonade,
I put on my disguise.

Now in Superhero mode
I dash from place to place.
Sneaking up on criminals
and farting in their face.

Recycling duties

When I'm off to bed I take
my pants and have a sniff.
They might last another day,
depending on the whiff.

Gas leak

Gas flew from my bottom,
swift as swift can be.
Nearly blew my pants apart
the smelly escapee.

Poop-de-loop

Did a roller coaster poo,
it really was quite smelly.
Did it on the loop-de-loop.
It landed on my belly.

Boulder ring

Climbing walls is really tough,
it's almost like an art.
When I climb up high enough,
I like to drop a fart.

Special friend

Farted in a little box and
tied it with a bow;
wrapped it up all prettily,
just to let you know.

You are very special and
I think I really care.
Don't know how to tell you so
accept my bottom air.

Party pooper

What a rotten stinker
sticking to my underside.
Can't escape the rotter,
even if I run and hide.

Chatting in the kitchen
I was feeling rather farty.
Tried to run away, but spread
the smell throughout the party.

Downward-facing bog

Many people tell me
doing Yoga's really ace.
When I go and try it,
I let rip into my face.

Bum scare over the rainbow

If you find a rainbow coloured
all the shades of brown,
find the end and dig a hole
as far as you can, down.

Soon you'll find a treasure chest
you'll want to rummage through.
Wear some gloves, for in the chest
you'll find a golden poo.

Stinkerbell

Have you smelt a fairy fart?

They smell like potpourri.

When I find a group

I let them fart all over me.

Birthday bake

I've a fart for every year that
you've been on the planet.
How I wish there was a way for
me to store and can it.

I would send the can for you
to sniff like fancy wine.
Potent farts would make you glad
that you're not ninety nine.

Public trans-poot

Did a little fart on the bus.

There's no one on it to make a fuss.

Lingering for far too long.

They'll know it's me
when someone gets on.

Passage of time

I used to skip on merrily,
farts just slipping out of me.

The trust we shared,
it was sublime,
but trust eroded over time.

Like tattered pants,
or an old hiking boot.
Oh, how I miss a care free poot.

Lethal ejection

If you choose a final meal
at your execution,
pick a stinky mix of grub and
leave some arse pollution.

Curl one in

If you play a football game when
you are full of gas.
You can try to score a goal with
vapours from your ass.

Hold your feet above your head,
line up your bum hole.
Fire a stinker at the ball and
blow it in the goal!

Missile launcher

My arse can be explosive,

I'm telling you the truth.

When I blow a bottom burp

My head goes through the roof!

Somme like it bot

There once was a fart called Tom,

Who briefly fought at the Somme.

It started to drop

Going over the top,

Then was blown away by a bomb.

Ring of fire

Are farts truly flammable?
I really have to know.
I spark them with a lighter
every time I have to blow.

It's left me with a blackened arse
and singeing round the cheeks.
The neigbours seem a bit concerned
about my painful shreiks.

"I'm fine," I say, "I'm lighting farts!"
but no one seems to care.
They're more concerned about the stench
that's hanging in the air.

The genuine sharticle

The farts in my bum
are feeling very glum.
They struggle to be heard,
when they're stuck behind a turd.

I wish that I could squeeze them out;
help them to depart.
But if I were to set them free,
I'd more than likely shart.

Leaky friday

Freely farting Friday is my
favourite working day.
All my belly bloopers can come
out and have a play.

Letting rip from nine to five,
breaking wind with pride.
Colleagues said I made it up and
took my desk outside.

Turdsmith

Have you heard the many words

For bottom burps that smell like turds?

Here's a common one to start.

Everybody knows a fart.

Breaking wind and flatulence.

Cutting cheese and crackers.

Bum bazooka, honker, guff,

underpant attackers.

Poot or toot, a trouser cough,

whoopee, whopper, rumble.

Cut one, drop one, booty bomb,

quacker, tummy tumble.

There is such variety,

describing every kind.

Try and use as many words

for gas from your behind.

Whiffy little blooper

Have yourself a
whiffy little blooper.
Let your bottom sing.
All year long you'll
see what joy your bum can bring.

Once again, there's a lingering
rear kindling
alight.

Noses twitch as they realise,
then you hear the cries
of plight.

Whiffy little blooper (cont.)

You will stop when it isn't fun
letting off a bun
that's brewed.

Faithful friends who are dear to us
will all jeer and call
you crude.

Someday soon we
all will be together,
talking over chow.
There will be a
moment where it fits somehow.

So have yourself a
whiffy little blooper
now.

The end

Here we are.

We've reached the end.

It's time to say farewell.

Got to run.

We'll meet again.

If you can stand the smell.

Thanks for reading!
You are supporting a very small
business by purchasing this book. If you
enjoyed it, I would be most grateful if
you could leave a nice review.
Many thanks for your support.
- E. B. Tooting

Printed in Poland
by Amazon Fulfillment
Poland Sp. z o.o., Wrocław
08 November 2023

ea84262a-4c3a-4c9d-9dc1-37f22263ddd5R01